AF093823

IT'S TIME TO EAT CHOCOLATE PUMPKIN CAKE

It's Time to Eat CHOCOLATE PUMPKIN CAKE

Walter the Educator

Silent King Books
A WhichHead Entertainment Imprint

Copyright © 2024 by Walter the Educator

All rights reserved. No part of this book may be reproduced in any manner whatsoever without written per- mission except in the case of brief quotations embodied in critical articles and reviews.

First Printing, 2024

Disclaimer

This book is a literary work; the story is not about specific persons, locations, situations, and/or circumstances unless mentioned in a historical context. Any resemblance to real persons, locations, situations, and/or circumstances is coincidental. This book is for entertainment and informational purposes only. The author and publisher offer this information without warranties expressed or implied. No matter the grounds, neither the author nor the publisher will be accountable for any losses, injuries, or other damages caused by the reader's use of this book. The use of this book acknowledges an understanding and acceptance of this disclaimer.

It's Time to Eat CHOCOLATE PUMPKIN CAKE is a collectible early learning book by Walter the Educator suitable for all ages belonging to Walter the Educator's Time to Eat Book Series. Collect more books at WaltertheEducator.com

USE THE EXTRA SPACE TO TAKE NOTES AND DOCUMENT YOUR MEMORIES

CHOCOLATE PUMPKIN CAKE

It's time to eat, oh, what a treat,

It's Time to Eat
Chocolate Pumpkin Cake

Chocolate Pumpkin Cake so sweet!

The smell drifts out, it's warm and grand,

Come to the table, fork in hand.

The frosting's rich, the spices bright,

A little slice feels just so right.

Chocolate swirls and pumpkin glow,

A mix so yummy, you should know!

The cake is soft, it melts away,

A perfect bite to start your day.

With every chew, you'll smile and hum,

"Oh, Chocolate Pumpkin Cake, here I come!"

The whipped cream dollop on the top,

Makes every bite a happy stop.

One more taste, let's make it last,

This kind of treat goes by so fast!

It's Time to Eat Chocolate Pumpkin Cake

The pumpkin gives a cozy hug,

And chocolate's like a cocoa rug.

Together they're the perfect pair,

A cake like this is super rare!

"Is it dessert or breakfast time?"

The answer is: it's just sublime.

So grab a plate and join the fun,

Chocolate Pumpkin Cake for everyone!

We'll eat it slow, we'll share a smile,

Let's sit and chat for a little while.

Each bite feels like a big embrace,

A yummy moment we can't replace.

So here's to cakes with flavors bold,

A slice to warm us when it's cold.

Chocolate Pumpkin Cake, hooray!

It's Time to Eat Chocolate Pumpkin Cake

A perfect treat for any day.

When plates are clean, and crumbs are few,

The memory stays, it sticks like glue.

Until next time, we'll dream and wait,

For Chocolate Pumpkin Cake on our plate!

It's time to cheer, it's time to clap,

For every bite's a tasty snap!

Chocolate Pumpkin Cake, so divine,

It's Time to Eat

Chocolate Pumpkin Cake

A treat to share and call all mine!

ABOUT THE CREATOR

Walter the Educator is one of the pseudonyms for Walter Anderson. Formally educated in Chemistry, Business, and Education, he is an educator, an author, a diverse entrepreneur, and he is the son of a disabled war veteran. "Walter the Educator" shares his time between educating and creating. He holds interests and owns several creative projects that entertain, enlighten, enhance, and educate, hoping to inspire and motivate you. Follow, find new works, and stay up to date with Walter the Educator™

at WaltertheEducator.com

www.ingramcontent.com/pod-product-compliance
Lightning Source LLC
LaVergne TN
LVHW010622070526
838199LV00063BA/5245